SCIENCE WORLD

RADIATION

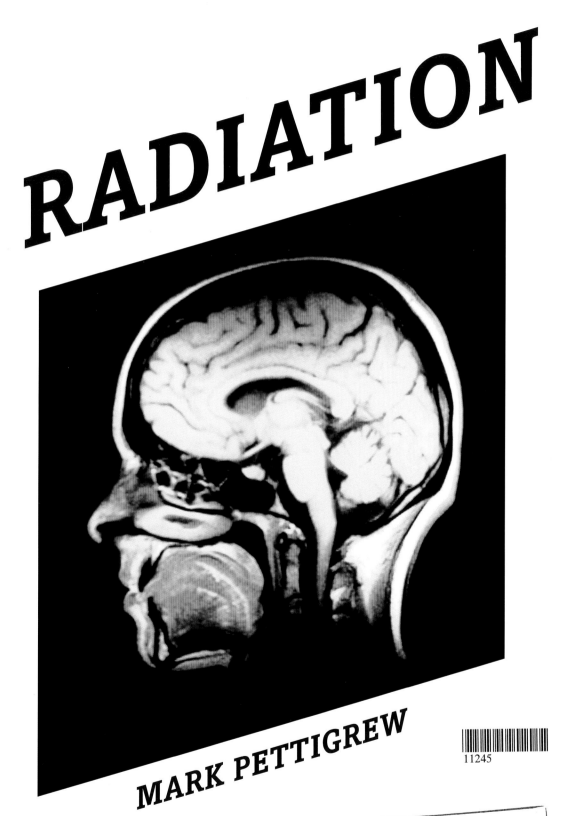

MARK PETTIGREW

Franklin Watts
London • Sydney

© Archon Press 2003

Produced by
Archon Press Ltd
28 Percy Street
London W1T 2BZ

New edition first published in
Great Britain in 2003 by
Franklin Watts
96 Leonard Street
London EC2A 4XD

Original edition published as
Simply Science – Radiation

ISBN 0–7496–5390–6

Printed in UAE

Editor: Harriet Brown

Designer: Pete Bennett – PBD

Picture Researcher: Brian Hunter Smart

Illustrator: Louise Nevett

A CIP record for this book is
available from the British Library.

2

CONTENTS

INTRODUCTION

Radiation is one of the main forms of energy. It is everywhere and it is essential for life on Earth. Rocks and minerals in the Earth, the Sun, and other objects in space provide natural radiation. It is also possible to produce artificial radiation for industrial, medical and research purposes. We can see or feel some types of radiation but many kinds, such as radio waves, pass right through our bodies without us even knowing.

Sunshine is the most familiar form of radiation. Without sunlight there would be no life on Earth.

In this book you will find out what radiation is and how the many different types of radiation occur. You will discover that each type of radiation has specific properties that are increasingly put to use in medicine, industry and even in your home.

Planet Earth receives radiation from outer space.

RADIATION IS EVERYWHERE

There are three main types of radiation – electromagnetic, cosmic and nuclear. The Earth is warmed and lit by radiation from the Sun in the form of electromagnetic waves. This light radiation from the Sun takes about eight minutes to travel the 149 million kilometres to Earth. Cosmic radiation mainly comes from exploding stars in outer space. However, the Sun also releases some cosmic radiation. Nuclear radiation is given off by certain radioactive substances. For example, the metal uranium produces nuclear radiation. Radiation surrounds us and we are constantly bombarded by it.

We can see and feel radiation from the Sun.

Radiation reaches us from the stars.

Nuclear power stations use radioactive metals to generate electricity.

WHAT IS RADIATION?

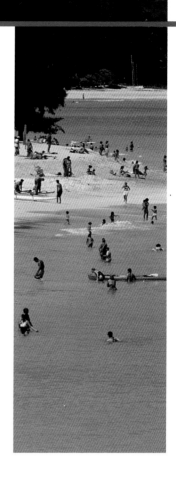

Radiation is energy travelling through space. Radiation usually travels in straight lines called 'rays'. On a fine sunny day, you can feel the Sun's rays warming your skin. When there are clouds in the sky, they block the Sun's radiation and you no longer feel the Sun's warmth.

Most scientists believe that the everyday radiation to which we are exposed is not harmful. However, large doses of radiation can be very dangerous. Some high power lasers produce a beam of light radiation that is intense enough to cut through sheets of steel. Yet most lasers do not transfer enough energy to be dangerous.

Heat as radiation

We can see the glow of an electric fire or of white hot coals. We can also feel the warmth, yet we cannot see anything travelling through the air to our bodies.

Most of the energy given off by an electric fire or a barbecue is in the form of invisible rays of radiation. It is the energy transferred by this radiation that we feel as warmth and see as light.

Low power lasers are used to create special lighting effects.

Radiation from the Sun can be seen around the edges of this cloud.

A BIGGER SPECTRUM

Light is the only type of radiation that humans can see. The light we see coming from the Sun is called 'white light'. By using a glass prism we can split up white light into a series of colours, called the 'visible spectrum'.

Scientists have discovered that visible light is only a small part of a large family of radiation, called the 'electromagnetic spectrum'. This includes types of electromagnetic radiation that we cannot see, such as gamma rays, X-rays, ultra-violet (UV), infra-red and radio waves. All these types of electromagnetic radiation travel through space at the same speed – 300,000 km per second, known as the speed of light.

The visible spectrum consists of a sequence of colours, from red to violet. The members of the electromagnetic spectrum also form a sequence, from gamma rays to radio waves. Gamma rays have the smallest wavelength and radio waves have the largest.

White light

Glass prism

White light split into a spectrum of colours

| GAMMA RAYS | X-RAYS | ULTRA-VIOLET (UV) RADIATION | LIGHT | INFRA-RED RADIATION | RADIO WAVES |

ELECTROMAGNETIC SPECTRUM

Right: Radio waves take several seconds to reach an astronaut in space.

INFRA-RED RADIATION

Just outside the visible spectrum, beyond red visible light, is infra-red radiation. Some of the energy from the Sun reaches us as infra-red radiation. These infra-red rays help to keep the Earth's atmosphere at a temperature in which we can live.

Anything warm gives off infra-red radiation. Very hot things such as electric fires and infra-red grills produce a lot of infra-red radiation. Some creatures, like tropical snakes, can actually detect their prey because they can feel the infra-red radiation from warm-blooded animals.

Earthquake victims buried alive under rubble can sometimes be found using a very sensitive infra-red camera. The camera detects the infra-red produced by their bodies.

Infra-red photographs taken from satellites show the temperatures of different parts of the landscape. Towns are usually warmer than the surrounding countryside, and rivers and lakes are usually a different temperature to land. The colours in the photograph below are not the actual colours of the landscape, but have been chosen to show the differences in temperature. Here, warmer areas are shown in blue, and colder areas are shown in red.

An infra-red photo of London: can you detect the warmer areas?

UV RADIATION

Ultra-violet (UV) rays are just beyond the violet end of the visible spectrum. The Sun produces UV radiation, and this is what damages skin and causes a suntan or sunburn. UV rays are invisible to our eyes, but they can be detected when they hit something 'fluorescent'.

Fluorescent substances, such as phosphor powder, react to UV radiation by producing visible light, which we see as a glow. By using mixtures of fluorescent substances, different colours of light are produced. Fluorescent substances are sometimes added to washing powder. This makes white clothes appear brighter by producing extra white light when UV rays from the Sun fall on them.

Visible light and infra-red rays from the Sun can pass through glass. This allows plants in a greenhouse to grow. UV rays are stopped by glass. So, people who work in greenhouses feel the Sun's heat all day but do not become suntanned or sunburned. It's important to protect yourself against the Sun's UV radiation by wearing sunscreen.

UV radiation is stopped by glass.

UV radiation tans skin.

Visible light and infra-red radiation travel through glass.

Fluorescent lights are used in brightly coloured advertising displays.

RADIO WAVES

Radio and television signals reach our homes as radio waves, a type of electromagnetic radiation. Radio waves can pass through walls and buildings. Without them there would be no mobile phones, radio or television.

Radio waves are used in radar systems. Radar is used to determine the position of a faraway object, the speed at which something is travelling and even to track storms. An air traffic control computer detects the position of a plane by sending pulses of radio waves towards it. As the radiation bounces off the plane, the time it takes to return to the aerial is measured by a computer. The computer can then calculate the plane's exact location.

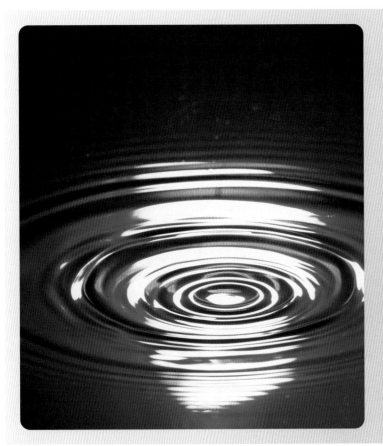

Radio waves spread out from a transmitting aerial in all directions, just like the ripples that appear when you drop a stone into a pond (left) or like light spreading outwards from a bulb. By placing a curved reflector behind a torch bulb, the radiation can be concentrated into a narrow beam. A beam of radio waves is produced in a similar way by the curved reflector of a radar transmitter.

Mobile phones also work using radio waves. They receive radio waves from, and transmit radio waves to, mobile phone towers. This allows people all over the world to communicate with each other.

Microwave ovens use special radio waves, called microwaves, to heat food. The microwaves penetrate food inside the microwave oven. Microwaves are absorbed by water, fats and sugars and converted into heat. However, microwaves are not absorbed by most plastics, glass and ceramics which explains why the oven itself doesn't get hot!

Microwave ovens use radio waves to heat food.

Radar signals are used to locate large, faraway objects.

X-RAYS

X-rays are a high-energy form of electromagnetic radiation. They are produced naturally by the Sun, but the X-rays we use are created artificially. X-rays can pass through many of the substances that stop light. They can pass through skin and cloth, but are absorbed by substances like bone and metal. X-ray cameras are used in hospitals to examine broken bones, and in airports to check for hidden weapons.

It is quite safe to have an X-ray photograph taken occasionally. However, large quantities of X-rays can damage the cells in our bodies. The people who take X-ray photographs hundreds of times each week stand behind a screen to avoid the harmful effects of radiation.

An X-ray camera produces X-rays, which are directed towards a piece of photographic film. The more X-rays that hit the film in one place, the darker the film becomes in that place. The object to be examined is placed between the source of X-rays and the film. X-rays are absorbed by bone, so very little radiation passes through the bone to the film behind and it remains white or pale grey in these areas. X-rays pass easily through skin and flesh, with only a little being absorbed, and the film behind turns dark grey or black. This produces a kind of 'shadow' picture of the bone on the film.

Right: X-rays can produce a picture of a human skeleton.

19

RADIOACTIVITY

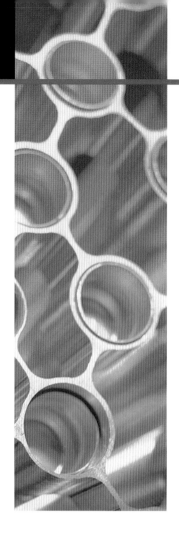

Everything is made up of atoms. An atom itself is made up of a tiny nucleus, surrounded by electrons. In most substances, these atoms remain unchanged because their nuclei remain stable. But some substances, like radon gas and uranium, have unstable nuclei which naturally give off radiation. These substances are 'radioactive' and the energy they produce is called 'nuclear radiation'.

Radioactive fuel, such as enriched uranium, is used in nuclear power stations. The fuel is placed in a series of fuel rods in the nuclear reactor. As the fuel is used, it produces a great deal of radiation. Thick layers of lead and concrete surround the reactor to protect the environment.

Radioactive waste is transported in specially designed containers for safety.

The decaying atom

The nucleus of an atom is made up of protons and neutrons. Protons carry a positive electric charge; neutrons carry no charge. Electrons circle around the nucleus. They carry a negative charge. The charges of the electrons exactly balance the protons.

In the atoms of a radioactive substance, the nucleus carries too many or too few neutrons and this makes it unstable. In order to get rid of this instability, bursts of radiation are produced from the nucleus.

This radiation is sent out as alpha particles, beta particles or gamma rays. This process of giving out radiation is known as radioactive decay. The radioactive atom naturally changes into another atom during this process.

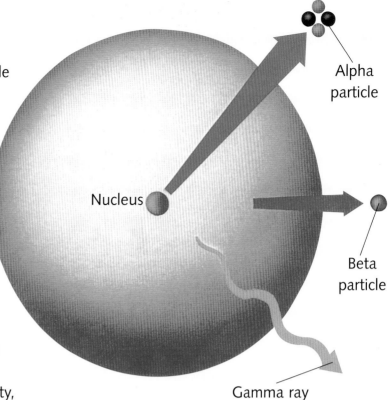

Nucleus

Alpha particle

Beta particle

Gamma ray

Absorption of particles

Alpha particles aren't very penetrative. They are stopped by a sheet of paper. Beta particles are a hundred times more penetrating than alpha particles, but they can still be stopped by a sheet of aluminium. Gamma rays are very penetrative, and it takes a thick sheet of lead to stop them.

Gamma rays

Beta particle

Alpha particle

Paper   Aluminium   Thick lead

DETECTING RADIOACTIVITY

Scientists measure the amount of radioactivity in a substance by counting the number of atoms that decay and so produce a burst of nuclear radiation. To do this, they use a Geiger counter, a sensitive instrument that can detect small amounts of radiation.

However, no matter how much radioactivity a substance has to start with, we find that half this radioactivity is lost after a certain amount of time. We call this period of time a 'half-life'. The half-lives of different radioactive substances range from less than a second for extremely unstable substances, to several thousand million years.

Half-life

Imagine deciding to drink half of what is in a glass of water every day. After one day there would be half a glass of water left. The next day you drink half of this, leaving only a quarter. After three days there would be an eighth left. In this example, the half-life of the water in the glass is one day: the time taken to halve the contents of the glass.

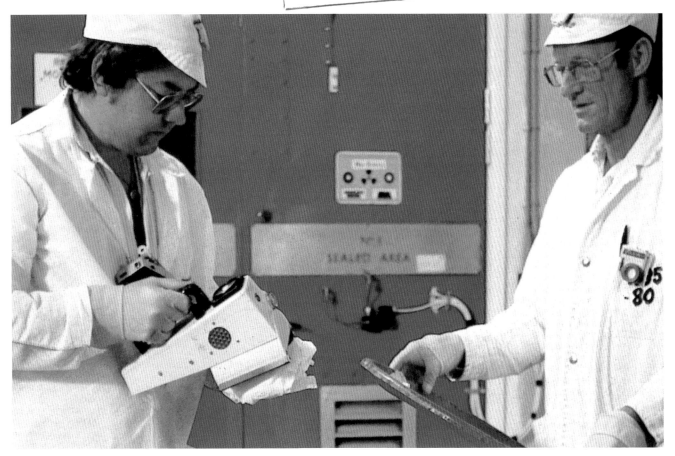

A Geiger counter is used to measure the radiation level from waste materials.

Soldiers wear protective suits and masks when they are at risk from dangerous levels of radiation.

NUCLEAR ABSORPTION

Alpha, beta and gamma are all very energetic types of nuclear radiation. When they pass through a substance, they can remove its outer electrons. This leaves atoms with a positive charge. Charged atoms are known as 'ions'.

Everything that alpha, beta and gamma rays can do depends on their ability to 'ionise' a substance. This is how they transfer energy from one place to another. As alpha, beta and gamma rays pass on their energy to a substance, they themselves are absorbed. Alpha and beta particles are more easily absorbed than gamma rays. Gamma rays can penetrate thick steel before they are finally absorbed by lead or concrete.

Beta particles are used in industry to measure the thickness of a thin sheet of metal. As the metal is produced it passes between a source of beta particles and a Geiger counter. The amount of beta radiation that passes through the metal is very accurately measured by the Geiger counter. The thinner the metal, the more beta radiation is detected. This information is used to control the thickness of the metal produced.

Geiger counter

Metal

Rolling mill

Source of beta particles

Carbon dating

Carbon dioxide in the air contains a small amount of radioactive carbon. All living things contain a little of this radioactive carbon: trees and plants take up the carbon dioxide from the air, and animals eat the plants. Living things all contain the same percentage of radioactive carbon.

For example, when a tree dies it stops taking in radioactive carbon. The radioactive carbon in the tree decays and isn't replaced. The percentage of radioactive carbon in the tree goes down. Radioactive carbon has a half-life of 5,700 years. The age of the tree can then be calculated by measuring the amount of radioactive carbon that is left.

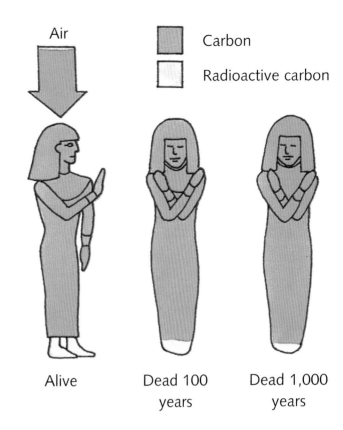

Air

■ Carbon

□ Radioactive carbon

Alive

Dead 100 years

Dead 1,000 years

Carbon dating shows that this Egyptian mummy is over 2,000 years old.

USES OF RADIOACTIVITY

The fact that radiation can kill living cells is often used to our advantage. Gamma rays are used to kill bacteria and viruses that cause disease. This is called 'sterilisation'. Medical equipment is often sterilised using gamma radiation. Gamma rays are also used in the treatment of cancer by killing the dangerous cells in the body.

Small amounts of radioactive substances, called 'tracers', can be put into a person's body. As they travel through the body, the radiation they give off can be detected. In this way, we can find out if the person's body is working normally.

Equipment used in surgical operations is sterilised by gamma rays before it is used.

This patient is undergoing a nuclear medical procedure.

MAKE YOUR OWN DISPLAY MODEL

Different types of radiation can pass more easily through certain substances than others. Radio waves can pass through buildings but are stopped by water. Light rays from the Sun pass through great depths of water until they are absorbed; the ocean floor is often completely dark.

Follow these instructions to make your own display model to show how some types of radiation are absorbed. By turning the disc you can see that X-rays pass through your hand and aluminium but are absorbed by lead. Can you see which ray penetrates most?

Making the model

Trace the drawings on the opposite page. Then transfer each tracing onto a piece of card. Label each piece of card as shown and colour in. Cut out the cards and also the shaded areas on disc (A).

Hold the pieces of card together with a drawing pin. When you turn the lower disc (B), the coloured ray will appear through the cut-out slits on disc (A) and match with the different names as they appear through the window.

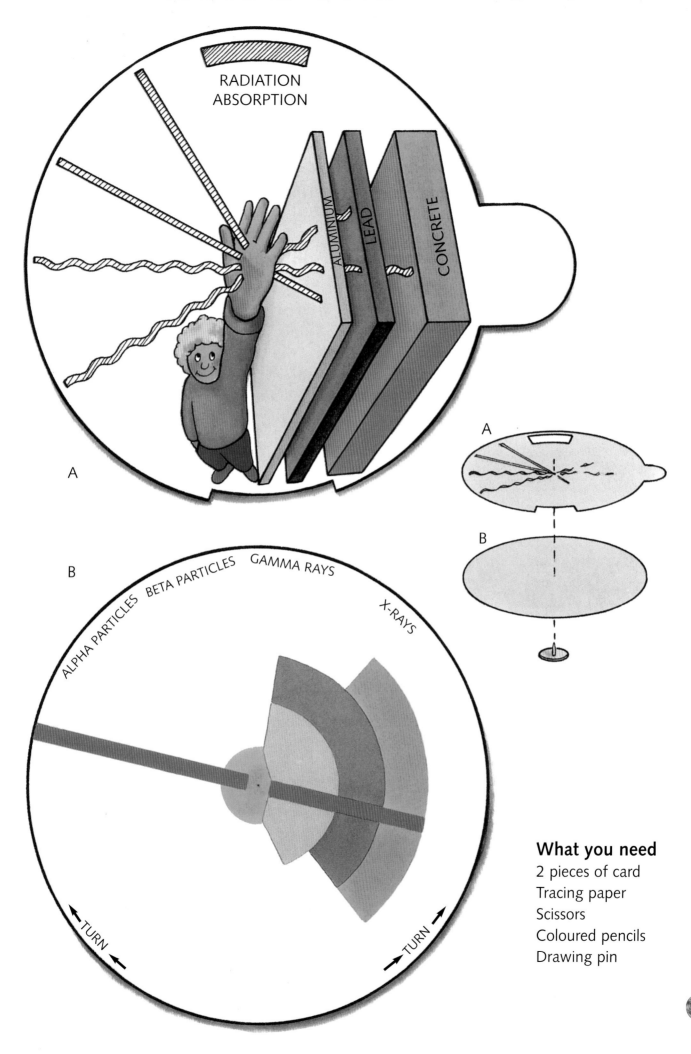

RADIATION ABSORPTION

ALUMINIUM

LEAD

CONCRETE

A

A

B

B

ALPHA PARTICLES   BETA PARTICLES   GAMMA RAYS

X-RAYS

TURN

TURN

What you need

2 pieces of card
Tracing paper
Scissors
Coloured pencils
Drawing pin

29

MORE ABOUT RADIATION

In high doses, nuclear radiation and X-rays are dangerous to all living things. However, our bodies are exposed to relatively harmless quantities of these types of radiation, most of which comes from natural sources.

There are radioactive substances present in the air, in our food and drink, in the ground and in buildings. We also receive cosmic radiation from outer space. Most X-rays are from man-made sources, and are used in medicine. Only a small amount of nuclear radiation is due to nuclear power stations and nuclear weapons. The diagram below shows the source and proportions of nuclear radiation and X-rays in an industrial society.

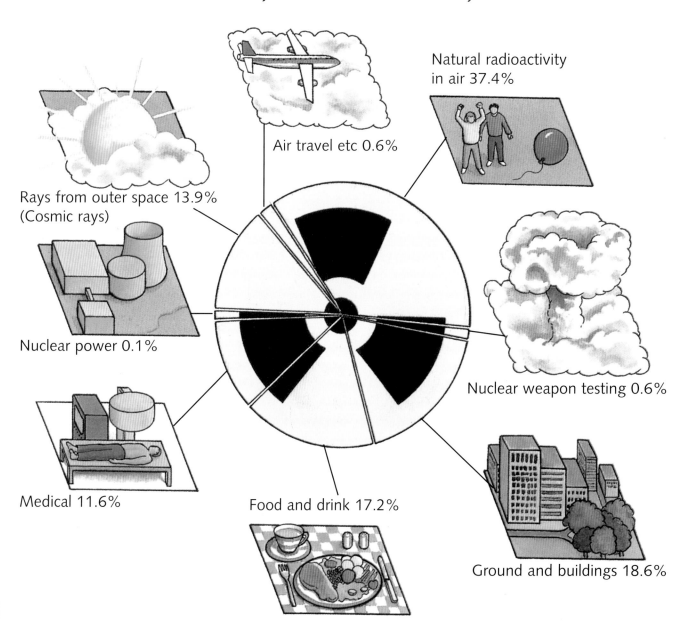

Rays from outer space 13.9% (Cosmic rays)

Air travel etc 0.6%

Natural radioactivity in air 37.4%

Nuclear power 0.1%

Nuclear weapon testing 0.6%

Medical 11.6%

Food and drink 17.2%

Ground and buildings 18.6%

GLOSSARY

Absorption
As radiation passes through a substance, it gradually loses its energy and is absorbed.

Decay
When the nucleus of a radioactive atom produces a single burst of nuclear radiation it is changed into the nucleus of a different atom. This is known as radioactive decay.

Electromagnetic spectrum
A large family of radiation which includes visible light, infra-red, ultra-violet, X-rays, radio waves and gamma rays.

Electrons
These orbit around an atom's nucleus. Every electron carries a negative electric charge.

Geiger counter
A sensitive machine used to detect small amounts of radiation. It counts bursts of nuclear radiation from atoms undergoing radioactive decay.

Half-life
The time taken for half the energy of a radioactive substance to be discharged by bursts of nuclear radiation.

Infra-red radiation
Invisible radiation just beyond red in the visible spectrum. Everything warm gives off infra-red radiation. It can be 'seen' by special infra-red cameras.

Ion
An atom usually has neither a positive nor a negative charge. But when an atom loses or gains an electron, it becomes positively or negatively charged and is known as an ion.

Neutron
In the nucleus of an atom are particles called neutrons. These never carry an electric charge.

Nuclear radiation
The nucleus of a radioactive atom gives out energy in the form of alpha and beta particles, and gamma rays. Because this radiation comes from the nucleus, it is called nuclear radiation.

Nucleus
The tiny central part of an atom. The nucleus contains protons and neutrons and is surrounded by electrons.

Proton
In the nucleus of the atom are particles called protons. These particles carry a positive electric charge.

Radioactive
Substances that are radioactive have their own energy because of their unstable nuclei. In the nucleus of a radioactive atom there are either too many or too few neutrons.

Ray
Energy spreading from a source, usually in a straight line. For example, a beam of light travelling from a torch contains many rays of light.

Stable
A stable substance is one that is not radioactive because it has a balance of neutrons and protons in its nucleus.

Ultra-violet radiation
Invisible radiation just outside violet in the visible spectrum. The Sun gives out ultra-violet radiation. Ultra-violet radiation can be 'seen' when it hits something fluorescent, such as phosphor powder.

INDEX

Photographic Credits

Abbreviations: l-left, r-right, b-bottom, t-top, c-centre, m-middle

Front cover main, back cover main, 16tr, 18tr — Digital Stock. Front cover mt, 1, 4tl, 4tr, 5tr, 6tl, 6b, 7t, 8tl, 10tl, 10tr, 11, 12tl, 14tl, 14tr, 16tl, 18tl, 19, 20tl, 22tl, 24tl, 26 all, 27, 28tl, 30t, 31t, 32t — Corbis. Front cover mb — Jennifer Swader/US Navy. 2-3, 4-5 b, 6tr, 8tr, 22tr, 24tr, 28tr — Photodisc. 7b — Personnel of Pierre 1985/NOAA. 8bl, 17t — Select Pictures. 9t — NASA. 9b — Roger Vlitos. 12tr — Corel. 13b, 20b — Science Photo Library. 15 — Flat Earth. 16bl — Comstock. 17b — Andrew Morrow/US Navy. 20tr — Paul Brierly. 23t — UKAEA. 23b — Angela Gonzalez/US Navy. 25b — Zefa. 28c — Cooper-West.